UNDER THE MICROSCOPE

OUR BODIES

Casey Horton

Gareth Stevens Publishing
MILWAUKEE

For a free color catalog describing Gareth Stevens Publishing's list of high-quality books and multimedia programs, call 1-800-542-2595 (USA) or 1-800-461-9120 (Canada). Gareth Stevens Publishing's Fax: (414) 225-0377. See our catalog, too, on the World Wide Web: http://gsinc.com

Library of Congress Cataloging-in-Publication Data

Horton, Casey.
    Our bodies / by Casey Horton.
      p. cm. – Under the microscope)
    Includes index.
    Summary: Presents a human hair that resembles a tree trunk, bones filled with as many holes as a sponge, tunnels in the skin for sweat to pass through, and other microscopic marvels of the human body.
    ISBN 0-8368-1601-3 (lib. bdg.)
    1. Histology–Atlases–Juvenile literature. [1. Body, Human–Miscellanea.
2. Microscopy.] I. Title. II. Series.
QM557.H67   1997
611'.018–dc20   96-34487

First published in North America in 1997 by
Gareth Stevens Publishing
1555 North RiverCenter Drive, Suite 201
Milwaukee, WI 53212 USA

© 1997 by Brown Packaging Partworks Ltd., 255-257 Liverpool Road, London, England, N1 1LX. Text by Casey Horton. All photos supplied by the Science Photo Library, except page 29: Frank Lane Picture Agency. Additional end matter © 1997 by Gareth Stevens, Inc.

Printed in the United States of America

1 2 3 4 5 6 7 8 9 01 00 99 98 97

CL
10/97

CONTENTS

HAIR TODAY

Human hair is made of a tough and shiny material called keratin. Each hair grows from a root in the skin that is shaped like a tiny onion. The root adds keratin to the bottom of the hair, and this pushes the rest of the hair up a tube called a follicle. By the time the hair reaches the surface of the skin, it has become hard and springy. Human hair usually grows less than 5 inches (12.7 centimeters) per year. Each hair falls out after three to five years. In most cases, human hair does not reach more than 2 feet (.6 meters) in length.

Looking like sticks surrounded by rose petals, human hairs sprout from dry, flaky skin on someone's head. The overlapping scales of keratin are also visible.

THE HAIR THAT GOT AWAY

- Some people's hair keeps growing longer and longer. The longest hair ever measured belonged to an Indian monk, whose hair grew to 26 feet (8 m)!
- The longest beard ever measured was over 17 feet (5 m). The longest mustache was measured at more than 8 feet (2.5 m).

TINY VAMPIRES

Many insects feed like tiny vampires, sucking the blood of bigger animals. One of these insects is the head louse that lives in human hair. A louse can move from one person's hair to another's, so children often can catch lice from each other as they play. Lice can bite, but the bite doesn't hurt. It just itches. Lice lay eggs that are shaped like tiny bottles. Each egg attaches to a hair and is difficult to remove. The lice themselves cling tightly to hair, too. To get rid of head lice, use a fine-toothed comb and special shampoo.

This head louse is clinging to a human hair with its curved claws. The green oval shape is an egg. Head lice and their eggs are very difficult to remove.

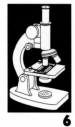

A LOUSY ELECTION

• Long ago, mayoral election customs in a certain Swedish town were unusual. Several men sat at a table and put their beards on the table. A louse was dropped in the middle. Whichever man's beard the louse crawled into became the mayor.

SWEATING IT OUT

The human body will not work well if it gets too hot, so humans have a special way of losing heat. When we overheat, pores in our skin develop drops of salty water called sweat. The drops lie on the surface of the skin and gradually turn to steam. This uses up some of the heat in the skin and cools us down. This system works best in dry air. If the air is moist, the sweat may not turn to steam quickly enough. This is why hot, humid weather feels more uncomfortable than hot, dry weather.

It may look like a crater on the moon, but this is actually a sweat pore on the palm of a person's hand. It leads from the gland that produces the sweat.

HOT AND SPICY

• In very hot places, such as Africa and India, people have learned that drinking hot tea and eating spicy foods actually help keep them cool. This is because the hot liquid and spices make them sweat!

8

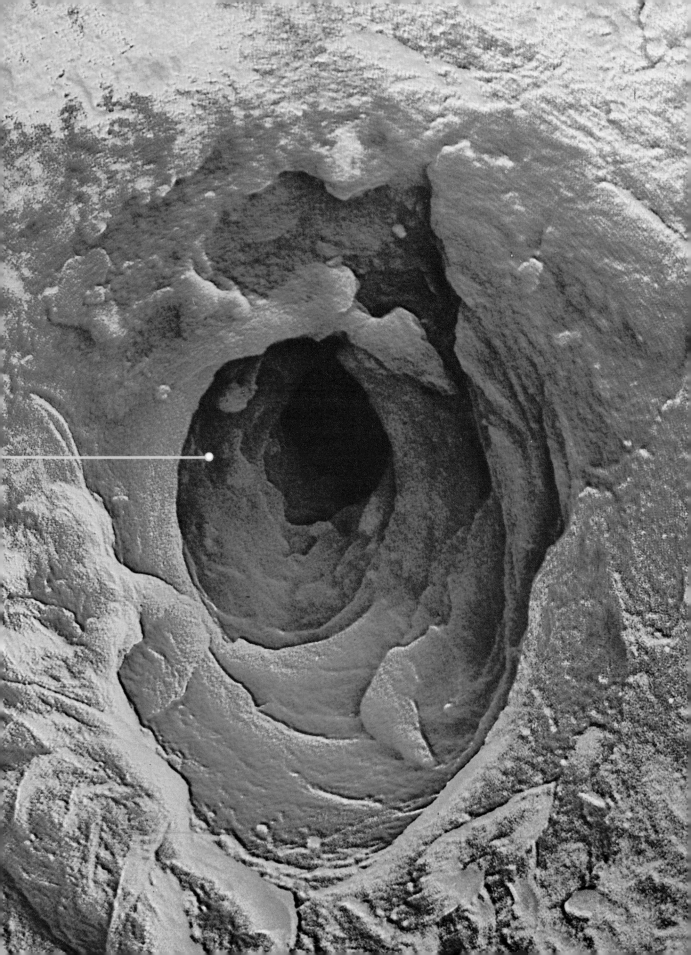

SKIN DEEP

Skin is very important for human survival. It protects human bodies from infections and keeps us from drying out in hot weather. Its tough outer coat resists damage. Our skin is constantly flaking away, taking dirt and germs with it. Beneath the outer coat is an even thicker inner layer. This layer contains hair roots, sweat glands, tiny blood capillaries, and nerves. The nerves are attached to special sensors that detect pain, pressure, heat, and cold. These sensors are located over the entire human body, but they are most numerous on our fingertips.

This view through human skin shows the outer layer (*red*) and part of the inner layer (*blue*). The large pale ovals are sensors that detect pressure.

DUST TO DUST

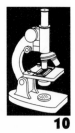

- The tiny flakes that fall from human skin drift around in the air and eventually settle as dust. Each of us sheds about a million of these flakes every forty minutes. Most of the dust that collects in houses is actually dead skin from humans and animals.

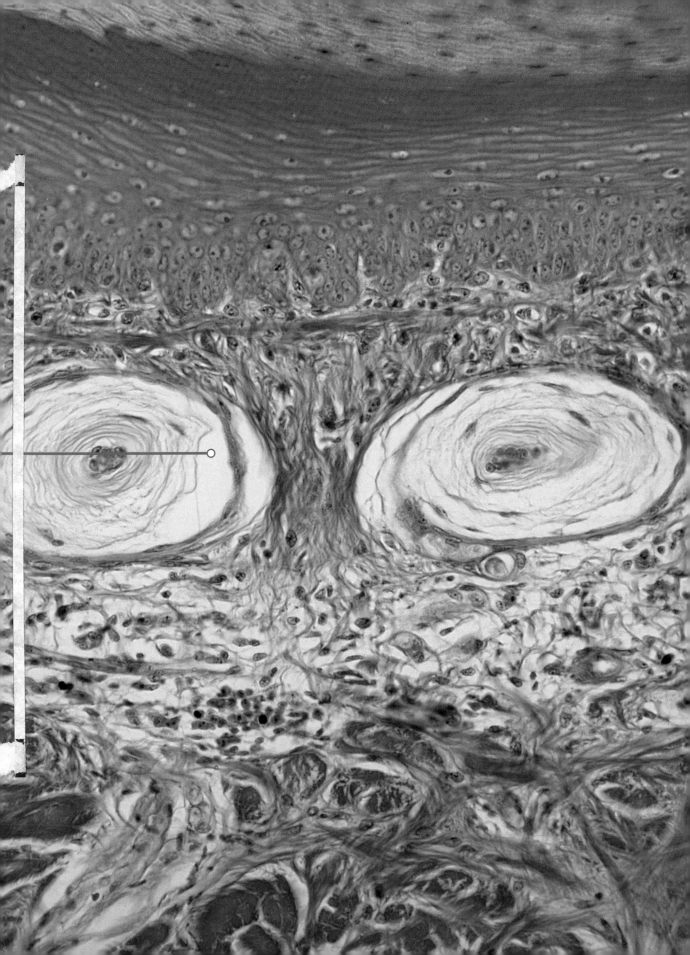

TASTEFUL TONGUES

The human tongue is covered with hundreds of tiny projections called papillae. There are two types — small and large. The small papillae have nerve endings that sense the texture of food. For example, they tell the difference between smooth and crunchy peanut butter. In between the small papillae lie larger, circular papillae. Each of these has a ring-shaped trough lined with taste buds. Taste buds are special sensors that distinguish between sweet, salty, sour, and bitter tastes.

Each of the large papillae on the tongue contains up to two hundred taste buds. The small papillae between the large ones contain sensitive nerve endings.

TASTE ZONES

• Each area of the tongue responds to a different taste. Sweet tastes are detected at the tip, salty tastes just behind the tip, sour tastes affect the sides, and bitter tastes are sensed near the back. Put some sugar, salt, and lemon juice on your tongue to see how your taste buds sense them.

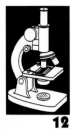

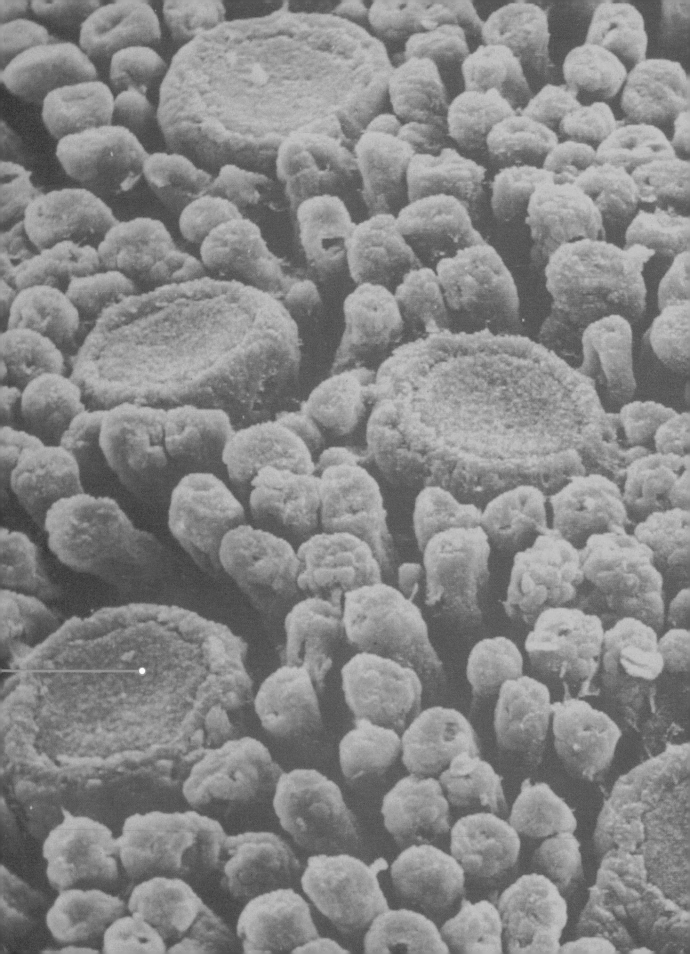

SPONGY BONES

The bones of children who are still growing are completely solid. As humans age, however, the bones become partly hollow so they are not so heavy. The hollow parts are filled with a substance called marrow. Marrow has the important job of making red blood cells. Red blood cells carry oxygen throughout our bodies. Furthermore, bones are often strengthened with a network of supports. These supports make the inside of a bone actually look like a sponge. Although bone is very hard and extremely strong, it is spongy in appearance.

The network of supports inside a bone keeps the bone rigid without making it heavy. The spaces between the supports are filled with a substance known as marrow.

BABY BONES

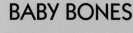

- A newborn child has about 350 bones in her or his body. As the child grows, many of these bones join together. That is why an adult has only 206 bones. Some of these are big, like the thigh bone. Others are tiny, like the bones inside the ear.

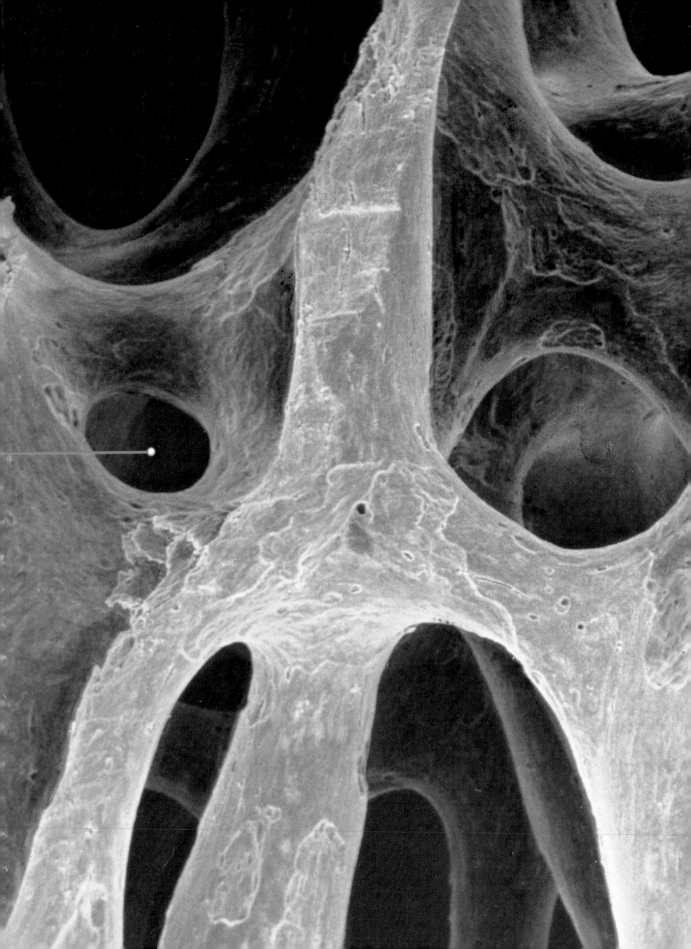

VIRUS INVASION

The tiniest life-forms on Earth are called viruses. They are parasites. This means they cannot survive on their own. They have to live inside other animals and plants. Viruses are so tiny they can actually live inside bacteria. Viruses place themselves into the cells that make up other living beings and force these beings to behave differently. Mostly, they make them produce more viruses, but they cause all sorts of other problems. Many of the world's diseases are the result of infection by viruses. These include smallpox, polio, mumps, measles, the common cold, and AIDS.

Magnified fifty thousand times, a virus looks more like a jewel than a dreaded parasite. This virus creates conditions similar to the common cold.

VIRUS VACCINES

- Diseases caused by viruses cannot be cured easily. A virus cannot be killed without killing the cells in which it lives. Some viruses can be prevented, however, with vaccines. Vaccines make the body kill the virus before the virus takes over any cells.

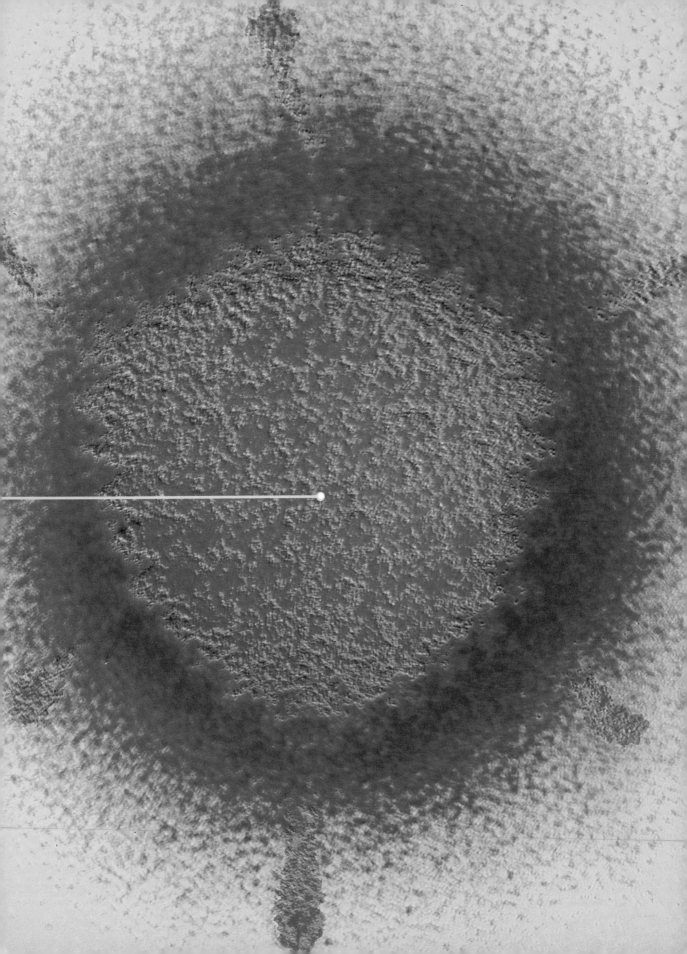

PERSONAL POWER

Just like the engine of an automobile, the human body needs fuel to work. Just as cars run on gasoline, our bodies run on glucose, a type of sugar made from food. Our bodies also need oxygen obtained from breathing the air. Glucose and oxygen are carried throughout our bodies in our blood. Glucose is dissolved in a liquid called blood plasma. Oxygen is carried by special red blood cells. Tiny tubes called capillaries carry blood to the muscles and other working parts. Glucose and oxygen are turned into energy that powers our bodies.

Red blood cells are just about to flow into a capillary on their way to a muscle. These blood cells carry oxygen throughout our bodies, giving us energy.

BLUE BLOOD

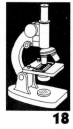

- When blood cells come in contact with oxygen, they turn bright red. When the oxygen is gone, they become dark blue-red. The color of blood indicates how much oxygen it is carrying. The blood in veins of your wrists has very little, so it looks blue.

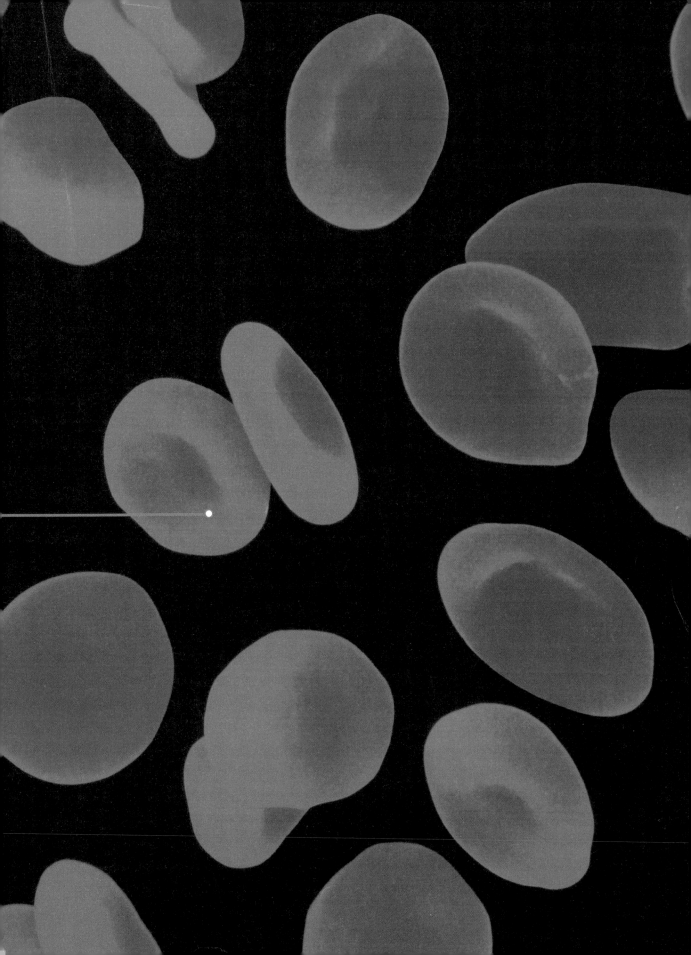

A CLOSE SHAVE

Human hair grows about .01 inch (.25 millimeters) on the top of our heads every day. This does not seem like very much, and you certainly cannot see the difference from day to day. The hair on a man's chin grows at the same rate. If the hair is dark enough, the growth can be seen after only a few hours. Men who shave usually have to shave every day, and some men shave twice a day. Beard hair is sliced off with a very sharp steel razor or an electric shaver. Before these were invented, all kinds of objects were used for shaving, including the teeth of sharks!

Under a microscope, beard hairs shaved with a razor blade look like sharpened logs of firewood. Hairs shaved with an electric shaver look torn and ragged.

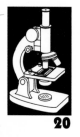

HAIR-RAISING BEARD

- The longest beard ever measured belonged to a Norwegian named Hans Langseth. When he died in 1927, his beard had grown to over 17 feet (5 meters). The beard was given to the Smithsonian Institution in Washington, D.C.

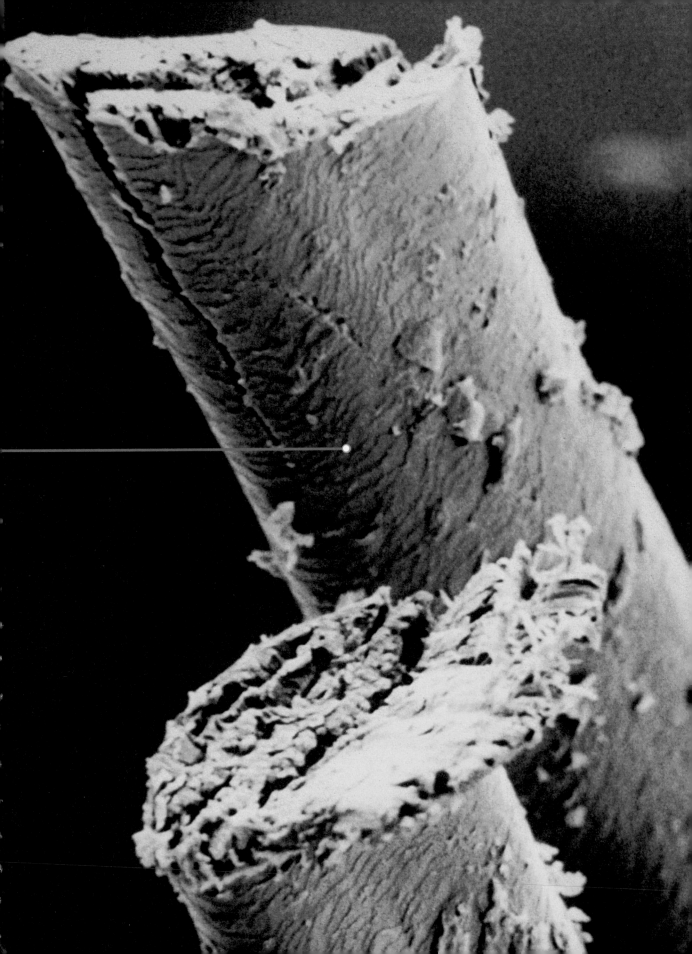

NATURAL BAND-AID

Blood has a built-in system for healing wounds to our bodies. If you cut yourself and are bleeding, large numbers of tiny cells called platelets glue themselves together and plug the cut. Meanwhile, a liquid protein called fibrinogen in the blood is converted into long strands of fibrin. These strands form a web over the wound that snares the larger blood cells and creates a clot. Eventually, the mass of cells, fibrin, and watery plasma sets into a hard scab. The scab stops bacteria from getting to the wound and causing infection. All of this enables the wound to heal.

Like fish caught in a net, these red blood cells have been trapped in a web of fibrin to form a clot. A scab will soon form to protect the wound until it heals.

CLOTTING CONDITIONS

- Some people have a condition called hemophilia that prevents their blood from clotting. If they cut themselves, the wound keeps bleeding.
- Some people suffer from blood clotting that takes place inside their bodies, blocking vital arteries.

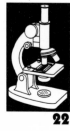

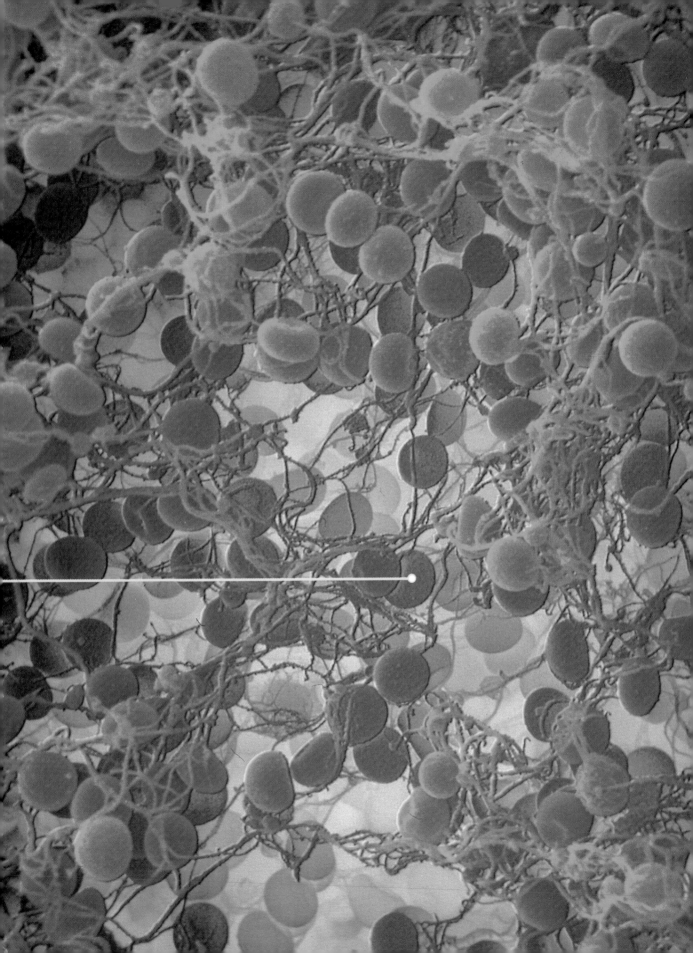

FROM FOOD TO FUEL

Food is of no value to our bodies until it is digested, or broken down into substances that can be used. Food is similar to a complex structure made from building blocks. In our bodies, the small intestine has the job of taking the blocks apart. The small intestine uses substances called enzymes to split the complex foods into simpler products, such as sugars. These are absorbed into the bloodstream through the small intestine and carried to the liver. Here, the products are turned into glucose that our bodies use as fuel.

The lining of the small intestine is covered in tiny, fingerlike projections called villi. Villi make the surface of the intestine bigger, increasing our ability to digest food.

A LONG JOURNEY

- The lengths of the small and large intestines of an adult human total about 25 feet (7.5 m).
- Most of our intestines are coiled up like a garden hose in the area of the stomach. The stomach is located just under the ribs.

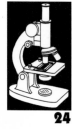

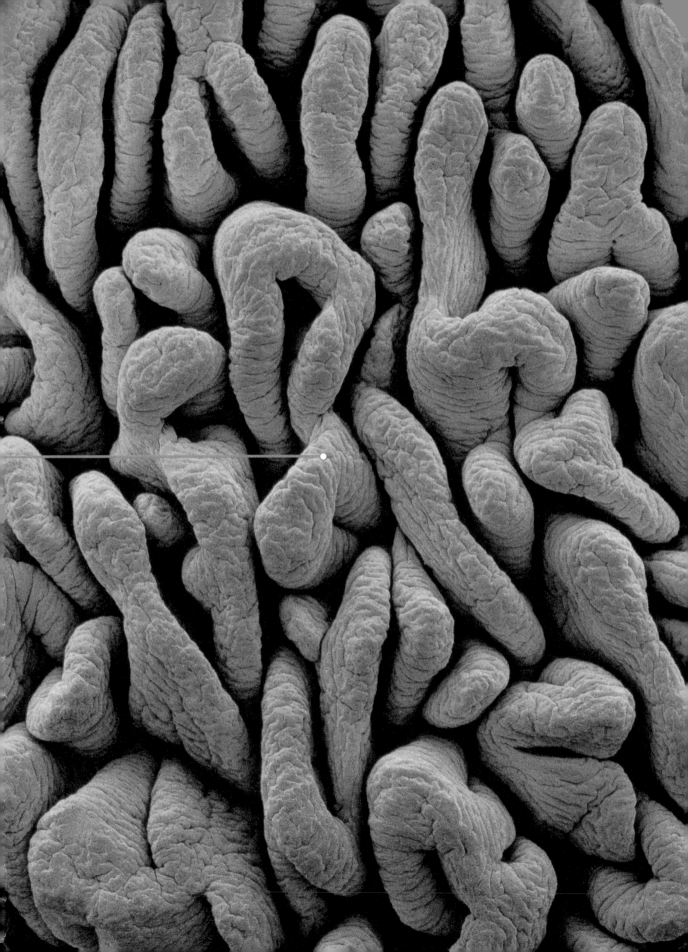

CREATING AN IMAGE

Our eyes are similar to miniature cameras, with lenses that can be focused to form a clear image. The image is projected onto a sheet of light-sensitive cells, called the retina, located at the back of each eye. The retina contains what are known as rods and cones. Rods are very sensitive, but they can detect only shades of light and dark, like in a black-and-white photograph. Cones are not as sensitive, but they respond to color. All the information gathered by these cells is sent down the optic nerve to the brain, where the signals are put together to form an image.

In each human eye, there are over 130 million rod cells *(pink and purple)* and 6 million cone cells *(blue)*. Information gathered by these cells is sent to the brain.

NIGHT VISION

• The cone cells in the human eye do not work in dim light. So as night falls, the color seems to drain out of our surroundings. Because this happens nightly, humans have become used to this effect and have adjusted to it.

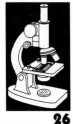

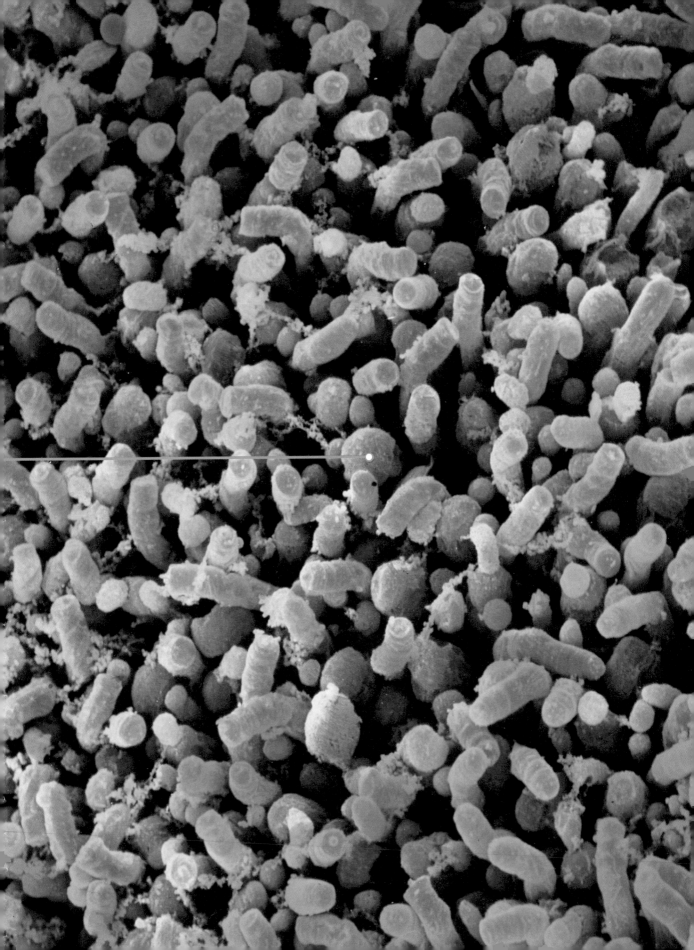

NATURAL COMPUTER

The human brain is similar to a complicated electronic circuit, wired with electrical nerve cells called neurons. Neurons process information. Messages are sent to muscles through motor neurons. For example, when you are in bright sun, a signal travels from your eyes to your brain. The brain then sends a signal to your hand to shade your eyes. But if you are suddenly dazzled by bright light, the signal goes directly to your eyelids and makes them blink. This is called a reflex. It occurs automatically, without your brain being involved.

This web of nerve cells is part of the natural computer called the brain. Each nerve cell has a central nucleus fringed with fibers that transmit messages to other cells.

REFLEX TEST

- Cross your right leg over the left. With the edge of your hand, strike your leg just below the knee cap. Your foot will jerk outward in an automatic reflex.
- Reflexes help the body react quickly in order to avoid injuries.

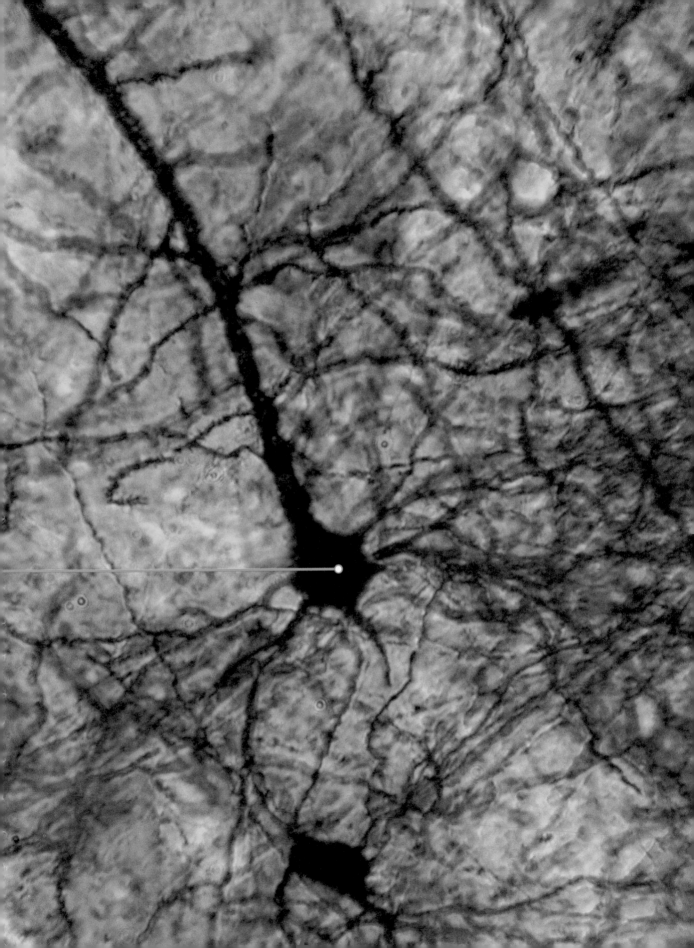

GLOSSARY

capillary: a very thin blood vessel.

enzymes: various kinds of protein molecules produced by the body. Some enzymes break down food.

fibrin: a silky substance that forms a web over a wound and clots the blood.

follicle: a tube in the skin containing a hair.

gland: a structure in the body that produces a special fluid.

glucose: a type of sugar used as fuel by our bodies.

keratin: the substance that makes up hair and fingernails.

marrow: the soft material that fills the insides of bones.

papillae: very small projections on the upper surface of the tongue.

plasma: the colorless, liquid part of blood.

platelet: the smallest blood cells. Platelets plug a wound prior to the formation of a blood clot.

pores: tiny openings in the skin.

taste buds: special sensors on the tongue that can distinguish between sweet, salty, sour, and bitter tastes.

vein: a tube that carries blood which has had most of the oxygen removed.

virus: the tiniest life-form found on Earth. Viruses are parasites, feeding off living plants and animals.

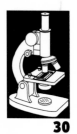

FURTHER STUDY

BOOKS

The Amazing Body. (Running Press)

Ask Isaac Asimov. How Does a Cut Heal?
Isaac Asimov (Gareth Stevens)

Bacteria and Viruses. Leslie J. LeMaster (Childrens)

The Children's Atlas of the Human Body.
Richard Walker (Millbrook)

The Human Body and How It Works.
Angela Royston (Random)

The Super Science Book of Our Bodies. Graham
Peacock and Terry Hudson (Thomson Learning)

Your Body. Linda Schwartz (Learning Works)

Your Heart and Blood. Leslie J. LeMaster (Childrens)

VIDEOS

Bacteria and Health. (AIMS Media)

Human Body Systems series. (Barr Films)

*Making the Unseen Visible. Images and Things
series.* (Agency for Instructional Technology)

Microbeasts and Disease. Scientific Eye series.
(Journal Films and Video)

*What's Inside Your Body? Children's Video
Schoolhouse series.* (I.J.E. Book Publishing/
Kid Stuff)

INDEX

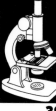